The hungry air

Walleah Press
PO Box 368
North Hobart
Tasmania 7002 Australia
ralph.wessman@walleahpress.com.au

Cover image: Rachael Wenona Guy

ISBN: 978-1-877010-90-3

The hungry air

Rachael Wenona Guy

Contents

Thread — 1

Visitation — 3
Thread — 4
These hands — 5
Doppelgänger — 7
Arboretum — 9
Dismantling — 10

Growing pains — 13

The fall — 15
Kings meadows — 16
Errand — 17
An inconsolable child recalls her transgression — 18
Discoveries — 19
First doll — 21
Flowers — 23
Immutable and everlasting — 24
Growing pains — 25
Imposter — 26
Bannister — 27
Understorey — 28
Necromancer — 29
All the pretty corpses — 30
Robe — 31

Archipelago 33

Exposure 35
Cape Barren Island 36
Civilisation 38
Vansittart Island 39
Keepsake 40
Hunger 42
Night 43
Day's end 44
Gannet 45
Fright 46
Intimate apparel 47
Bide 48
Packed lunch 49
The Final Night 50
Beyond Reach 51
The house is burning 52
Archipelago 53

Eulogy 55

Vitamin C 58
Cardboard Box 60
Colouring In 61
Sunbathing 62
Big Teeth 63
Drawing 64
Spider 66
Blizzard 67

Keening 69

Whenever it Rains 71
Glove Puppets 72
After the Fire 73
Rising 74
The Fact 75
Keening 76
The Hungry Air 77

Acknowledgements 80

For my mother Molly Guy 19.8.1948 – 30.12.2019

Thank you for a life-time of memories, these vivid dark pearls of recollection for which I keep diving.

So glad you were able to read these poems.

Thread

Visitation

She came to me one night. Her straw-coloured hair reeked of forty years of neglect, her moth-eaten jumper exposed a thin shoulder. She stared at me, a rueful gaze assessing the middle-aged woman we had become.

What do you want? I asked, but we remained silent. I tried to touch but could not get close, her restless limbs and scuffed knees just out of reach. Her nimble mind moved fast, such fickle tangents.

We faced one another. I wanted to see the resemblance between us, but could find little likeness.

Outside the night was clear and still — the sky immense, stars pointing to our transience. Inside my head, squalls rolled in. She was beginning to lose definition — her face becoming a shadow, the outer edge of her wild-grass-hair, a thin, dirty halo.

I'm sorry, I said, knowing I'd let us down. I had become a numb somnambulist pushing through our days and hours, attending to the mundane. Childhood had receded in all its hope and boast — a radiant naivety, never to be reclaimed.

At dawn, I woke. She was nowhere to be seen. Yet somewhere, deep inside this grown body — the cooling embers of her curiosity.

Thread

I am woven
from spools of your DNA –
your toes, your voice,
the shallow bowl of your pelvis.
Your love of language,
bent for the macabre.
Your fatalism and this illness
which has no name.

Our bodies shrink from the world,
aberrant nervous systems,
excitable and capricious –
this fragile cohesion threatening
to unravel at any moment.

The spasmodic dance of our musculature
jerks us awake each day –
I sense you stirring in a distant bed,
limbs hesitant, nerves twitching,
a new pain rising somewhere in the wayward
warp of your body.

All my life I have disavowed our likeness,
but as the years gather our identities coalesce.
We are cut from a line of brittle women,
who raged at the incessant unpicking
of misfiring synapses and vivid pathologies –

women who, nonetheless,
wove glittering reams of stories
on broken looms.

These hands

look like mine.

The narrow thumb
bent as a comma,

rolling tilt of index finger,
shape of fingernail.

But these hands
belong to my father.

It strikes me as I watch him write,
the way the digits grasp the pen,

or when I glimpse him
turning pages of a book,

ruffling the coarse
neck of a neighbour's dog.

These actions and gestures
could be mine.

I recognise the logic of those hands.
The astute and supple fingertips

moving as if they had some intrinsic
will of their own.

These hands remind me
I am an assemblage,

these fingers and palms,
maps of inheritance,

the stubborn re-arising of flesh
across generations.

Their delicate cursive
has trailed the pages of my life,

my father's and my father's father.
With these hands

I carry the sentence,
the ampersand,

full stop.

Doppelgänger

I see you from time to time.

Middle-aged and handsome in an unconventional way, you exhibit an air of a shy curiosity. Your face might be smooth or weathered, your hair wavy and greying.

In your hand hangs an old felt fedora. Occasionally you wear exquisite glasses, the lenses lightly greasy, or sharply clean. A discrete square of duct tape might hold a wayward frame in place. Or not.

You are out of time – a little atavistic somehow. A leather satchel hangs from one shoulder. You might be wearing European sandals – and just once I caught sight of your clean bare feet, quietly flagrant beneath linen hems amidst the formal dress.

You can be found lingering in a museum or art gallery – alone, arms folded, deep in reverie – or writing in a journal somewhere – a cafe, park or library. Sometimes you are simply sitting, watching.

You are not my father or my brother. You are not my lover or friend.

When I see you, I feel a frisson – I think,
"There I am – the *real me*. Living my *actual* life."

Sometimes I wait for you to return my gaze, expecting a mutual recognition. But it never comes. Instead you look unsettled, wonder why a strange woman is gazing so intently, perhaps intrusively in your direction. Does she know you?

All my life I've waited to grow into you. But I will never look in the mirror and see your face, nor wake to the economy of your male form. My wardrobe doesn't hold your clothes, my house is not your home – my skin does not contain you.

You are the man I am not becoming.

Arboretum

For A.J.

We were sitting on the hill when you said,
There are no grey hairs on the back of your head — only your crown.
A spike of existential strangeness ran through me
as I visualised you looking at the back of me.
Suddenly, I sensed the circumference of my own head,
neat as a pebble. For a moment I occupied more than just
the shallow oval of my face. I said,
It makes me feel strange that you can see the back of my head.

You replied, *I feel like that about my skeleton —*
these hips, these wrists, these long unwieldy shins.
You unfolded yourself as you spoke — the origami
of your structure, angular in the afternoon sun. Behind you,
russet trees marched single-file up-hill against a darkening ridge.
The wind picked up. Your shirt fluttered against your chest
like a beating moth. For a moment we were naked
in our radiant materiality. A man and a woman
at the arboretum.

Dismantling

I prise out tiny nails
driven into timber
a lifetime ago
or more —

I'm deconstructing
the workmanship
of the dead.

Freed of its broken frame,
the mirror bears imperfections
of a hand-hewn age.

The edge is crudely scored,
bevel asymmetrical.
Miniscule gaps break
the reflective surface.

Seeing my own reflection
on this oval plane I wonder
how many others have appeared here?

What private moments of nakedness
or apprehension have played out
on this glassy retina?

How many faces have peered into
the mystery of themselves;
open pores, secret pockets
of dimpled flesh? The stocking,

the new dress. The first grey hair,

the last. Bodily vacillations,
shifting across decades.

I am just one apparition reflected
on this gleaming surface,

one of many
soft and temporary things.

Growing Pains

The Fall

I remember my mother
fallen there in the darkest
reaches of the corridor.

Her plangent crying, so like a wounded animal,
tousled mass of curled hair
spilling across the floorboards in a slit of light.

She was sobbing into the crook of her arm,
clutching an ankle, writhing with a pain
I could not decipher.

I tried to pat her, tidy the damp strands
of hair stuck to her face, but she wailed
and growled and shrank from my touch.

I could not comfort her, so I just stood there —
clutching the bunched hem of my dress
like an unlaid wreath.

Kings Meadows

In a cage in the kitchen an orange canary flits ceaselessly,
seed husks and dander eddying in its wake.

The small wire door is open now,
but still the bird refuses its freedom.

The girl in the tree house is anxious. She can see
her parents through a window — they're almost touching.

Her parents seldom bicker. Instead a thin,
pervasive stream of contempt runs between them.

All about the house, unmet expectations are heaped
in corners, eating the walls like rising damp.

~

The girl dreams of her mother
on a mortuary slab. Bending to kiss

the cold body, she tastes boiled carrot.
Ever after, she refuses to eat it.

~

In the lounge room, curtains are perpetually drawn.
the couch is flocculent, second-hand.

A long time ago, the girl's auntie bled profusely
on the upholstery in a moment of illicit teenage passion.

The couch was new then, pride of place. Frantically
she scrubbed at the stain, tried to make it disappear.

To this day, the stubborn trace remains.

Errand

do you remember

    the big yellow dog that knocked you down and
             bit your scalp as you walked
                    to the corner store?

you fell heavily, legs splayed stiffly as a toppled doll,
        dress hitched high, dirtied and immodest,
           blonde hair stiff with dog spit,
                snap, snapping of jaws —

the owner sat on his verandah and laughed.

        still, you fulfilled your errand —
           bought milk and bread.

the next day mother insisted
      you walk past the dog again.
         be brave, she said,
          and armed you
           with a thin black umbrella.

        the dog came,
          you struck out.

you thought your mother
      the most beautiful woman in the world,
        her pale, tweed trench coat cinched at the waist;
        dark hair, tangled as the shadowy
          understory of the tea tree —

she was never going to die.

An inconsolable child recalls her transgression

I wore a yellow belt with them,
white turtleneck skivvy and pigtails tied with elastic.

New corduroy flares
the colour of burnt caramel.

In my secret corner of the garden,
I knelt down and stroked the plush, delicate pile.

Rubbed flat, it had the slick of wet animal pelt;
brushed up, the colour was luxurious as a pony's flank.

I took out some nail scissors and made an incision,
a tiny V in the thigh — a small arrow of skin peeked through.

How pleasing the feel of the fabric's brief resistance,
the cold metal nub of scissor blade nudging skin.

I snipped the other trouser leg. Two little flesh portals appeared.
I cut, cut again.

Soon my trousers hung in ribbons, broken tufts
of corduroy drifting in the grass.

I twirled in my shredded raiment,
relishing the air across my thighs —

tattered fabric flaring like maypole ribbons.
I was centrifugal, electric.

Discoveries

@5

I climb into the bath in my favourite
blue and white striped jumper.
Submerged, the net of wool becomes
a rank mantle, billowing about me,
hem undulating like the wings of a Manta ray
sucking my body down, down
towards the whining black maelstrom of the plug hole.

@9

Hiding in the chicken coop
in the furthest corner of the garden,
we pore over his father's stash of porn.
Ruddy and hirsute mysteries lie within the glossy pages,
colossal bodily terrain, foliaged crags.
Our own bodies are moon-stark, budding –
fingernails translucent as snail hatchlings.
He pulls down his shorts and offers me one buttock.
I bite the soft dough, then spit on the pavement walking home.

@11

She gives me an orphaned joey,
shows me how to feed him with the tapered
yellow teat of a small bottle.
Do not let him get cold she warns.

For one week I am an excellent mother.
Diligently I feed my baby, wipe his tiny anus,
swaddle him in squares of soft towelling.
Then one evening, impatient to play with my brother,
I finish feeding my tiny charge,
bundle him quickly into a loose nest of rag.
Reaching into the mound of cloth the next morning,
no skerrick of heat nor quiver of waking –
just the tiny grey corpse of my care.

First doll

*"… we were so busy keeping you in existence
that we had no time to grasp what you were."*
                                        Rilke

I combed the sticky platinum hair,
washed her unblinking face,
held the tiny fused fingers of her hand
between my thumb and forefinger.

But I was not satisfied.
She appeared to be a girl like me –
but was she?

I rummaged beneath her dress
for her hidden parts,
found only the smooth plastic girdle
of crotch bereft of cleft or sphincter –

only the faint imprint
of a manufacturer's mark veiled
there beneath her cotton pants.

Running the length of thigh and flank,
the thin line of her factory joining –
closest thing to a scar or blemish,
remnant of her two halves coming together.

But where was my maker's mark?

I lifted my dress, hunting for some trace
of my own moulding, that mysterious beginning
beyond memory or sensation,

and in the middle of my belly I found it.

The thing I possessed that my doll did not,
remnant connection between me
and the humid womb of my mother —

the small sealed mouth of my navel.

Flowers

As a child she collected them – the great dead men of history.
Grief's flowers pressed tight in the locket of the heart.

Searching the pages of biographies, she wanted to know
first how they died, *second* whom they loved.

She scanned the pages for any possibility of resurrection
and found it in the third person singular – each *'his'* and *'he'* tracing
the long-absent body. Embedded in the contours of print,

remnants of breath, volition and sweat.
He was… *He* possessed…*He* wept…
The revivification of the dead through language.

Sometimes she would tear a section off a page and carry it in her pocket.
It might read, "*He* was a very private man", or "There were great
possibilities always in the cavern of *his* soul",

and once,

"…there is something macabre and tragic in the fact that he
who burned so bright should have died at the age of a flower."

Immutable and everlasting

At seven years of age, I see a photograph
of Lewis Carroll. It shows him as a young man,
his soft face gazing down at the book he holds.

Dark hair frames his face. His hands
are graceful, skin without blemish.
I am besotted.

I imagine that, though long dead, he lies
underground, perfectly intact in his buttoned waistcoat,
face serene as a mirror. I am inflamed

by his demeanour and by the knowledge
that he cultivated child-friends. The possibility
of this reverence towards my childhood

reverberates across time. I feel an enigmatic frisson,
compose letters, promising I will be coming
to retrieve him. In my mind,

I rehearse bringing him up from the earth,
fresh as a rhizome, brushing crumbs of soil
off his Victorian frockcoat. In my daydream,

we are seated together at a table taking high tea.
I am on his lap, leaning against a velvet lapel,
his 20th century child-friend, his new Alice.

Propped in a chair, he is a most companionable effigy.
I drape his pale hand over my small shoulder,
brush his chin with an affectionate thumb.

His unblinking beauty is luminous –
scentless as a paper daisy,
immutable and everlasting.

Growing pains

came each night without fail,
a murmur in my shins

the secret, nauseating song
of bones elongating in the dark

soon the walls began to breathe,
in/out/in/out

I was pulled in,
sternum first – my small ribs

rising and falling in unison
with the room, skeleton becoming

creaking bedhead
and bow-legged chair

the door hovered like an invitation
but I could not leave

caught as I was,
a small moth pinned to night

my child-body, already
on its journey into the unknown

the one-eyed bear beside me
face-down and love-worn

the tiny voice inside my head,
mistaken for an adversary

Imposter

At my one-and-only birthday party   I turned eight,
cheated at   pin-the-tail-on-the-donkey   exhausted
    myself   with the thought   that   I was the most
                unpopular   person there.

    Waving   a pink balloon   I ran
        from one friend   to another
                    haunted by comparison whichever
                    way I turned –
prettier, kinder, smarter, nicer clothes,
                                lovable.

The next day at school I avoided   *all* the children
    who had been at my party for the shame
            I felt   at my own eagerness   to *please*
    for the pain   of watching   them play
                with one another –   happy
            with   or   *without*   me.

    At my one-and-only birthday party   I wasn't
                quite there.
            The presents piled in the corner
                            were bright decoys

        the girl running around in *my* skin
                            an *imposter* –
            her luminous smile
                    a brittle piñata.

Bannister

My small hand on its burnished surface,
cool and waxy to the touch, curling brass end caps
radiant as promises.

Sweeping down the staircase in a reverie,
nearly lunchtime, dreaming of the cling-wrapped sandwiches
in my blue lunchbox smelling of plastic and butter.

Down, down the stairs, bannister in my grip,
the shallow, hard steps pleasing beneath
my hard, black Bata shoes – playground in sight.

On the last step, the headmistress –
It is a school rule that children DO NOT touch the bannister –
to my office now!

I am struck five times on the back of each thigh with a cane.
Light puffs of air make my skirt flounce as if I were dancing.
The sting of wood on flesh shocks me into silence –

Bannister. Once, the smooth accomplice
beneath my palm –
now you hover by the stair, a dark splinter
reeking of furniture wax and authority.

Understory

My weapon was a short, smooth stick.
I tied a wallaby skin around my waist
with twine and loosened my plaits.

My best friend wore a long red dress
stolen from his mother's wardrobe.
Together we climbed the fence
and escaped into the wild.

Save me, he cried,
swooning against a tree.
He writhed and gasped, tossing his shining hair
and let out a long, high-pitched scream,
imagining the unseen assailant.

I sensed the terrible, dark, masculine shape
of his fear and wrestled it from him,
cutting the invisible ropes binding
his soft white hands.

Together we fled,
my cheeks daubed with earth,
his make-believe high heels catching
on fallen branches —

the hem of his flame-red dress snagged
on the tangled understorey
of his burgeoning.

Necromancer

She is an industrious child, knows charisma when she sees it. She draws. Papering the walls of her bedroom, portraits of Lord Horatio Nelson and Beethoven rendered in 6B pencil on cartridge paper. They are handsome, with square shoulders and firm lips, exaggerated hair and intense eyes. Close attention is paid to the details of Nelson's uniform, the pinned, empty sleeve, metal threads and silver spangles of his epaulettes.

While drawing Beethoven she listens to Moonlight Sonata – imagines she's hearing the cadence of his speech secreted between the intervals of notes, his breath rising and falling with the sombre arpeggios. She shades his breeches carefully with a smudged fingertip.

The little bowl of pencil shavings on her desk is overflowing. It smells of graphite and wood. Head down, she is whiling away her precious childhood hours growing her private gallery of immortals; each portrait, a kind of friend, each pencil stroke a small mark of defiance against forgetting.

All the pretty corpses

1984

Once, I showed an elderly woman a photograph I'd found in a magazine of an ice mummy. The young man's perfectly preserved body had been exhumed from a tundra, one hundred and thirty-eight years after his death. His eyes were open, forget-me-not blue.

My, she said, *there is such untold beauty in nature.*

Her enigmatic response stirred me. It was a form of bravery that I lacked — so I began my work.

Each night, I would take out the dead man's picture and look carefully at some small detail — his hands, bluish at the knuckle, one thumbnail detached, or his long dirty-blonde hair trailing damply from beneath a faded polka-dot scarf.

His inescapable deadness made me want to flee — but I kept looking, kept reaching for the limits of my capacity to love.

After looking I would fold the image over, slip it under my mattress. Stomach churning, neck pressed stiffly to pillow, I would gaze at the ceiling — think of all the pretty corpses lying unseen beneath us, silent as slippers.

Robe

Open the door.

There, pooled in dark recesses,
her secret feminine odour.
Hair, skin and breast.

Let the heavy tweed lapel of her jacket
brush your cheek. Blouses,
turtleneck sweaters and flared
trousers are piled in a mound.
Her rolled socks, threaded through with long
brown strands of her hair.
The wiry, animal part of her
escaped to the wilderness of this closet.

Next, climb into the upper reaches,
inhale the rich odour of timber drawers.
Thumb through her personal papers —
the indecipherable adult code of cursive
on blue lined notepaper.

Now, curl yourself deep within the mound
of clothing; nudge it, as if seeking succour.

Close the door.

Archipelago

Exposure

The island is exhuming its dead again,
paring back the earth, gust by howling gust,
'til they come rising in their wooden boxes,
hummed back to the surface
by the unrelenting song of gale.

Exposed in all their tat and disrepair,
hair spills through cracks in caskets,
fingernails jangle like loose change.
So many teeth and rags in these dunes,
another year, the dead laid out
like tarnished keepsakes.

There is no privacy in this place –
we, the living and the dead,
are all pared back
to stubborn flotsam and tattered rigging.
Patiently we rebury one another,
grain by recalcitrant grain.

Cape Barren Island

You're lying in a narrow bed
listening to island squalls.
The piano in the corner
smells of old felt and broken ivory.

Come dawn, Grandmother will be straddling
a milking stool, head to flank, squeezing
blood-warm milk from a greased teat.

In the kitchen a vat of oatmeal cooks.
Grandfather watches and stirs
as it cakes his patient spoon.

Dough rises in a ceramic mixing bowl –
a mysterious, viscous expansion,
belching beneath white muslin.

Outside in the windy field
a stillborn lamb
lies drying in its caul.

A wet calf staggers on trembling legs
while afterbirth protrudes from the heifer.
You can't name exactly what it is you're seeing –

only the sickly rising of your
childish incomprehension.

Daily, geese, goats, fish and fowl
are slaughtered, gutted, bled and diced –
entrails coiled in a bucket.

Plumes of dirtied feathers
eddy about the floor. Blood is a stubborn
substance, smelling of iron and endings.

You begin to cry — Uncle taunts,

This is life kid, we're all carrion
                    sooner or later.

Civilisation

Willow pattern cups, nesting on a silver tray,
a French soup terrine, Wedgewood figurine.
All her finest things on display.

This cabinet, a delicate museum,
upholding civilisation in a wild and barren place.

Outside, dunes are wearing away.
Winds howl across the Bass Strait.
The old blue healer barks by the tank stand.

Inside, the mirrored tiers of the cabinet shimmer —
spangled light moves across cool walls like sentience.
Above the mantelpiece hangs a large framed print of horses
galloping across a ford. The club lounge is humped as a camel.

We children kneel before this cabinet of wonders,
eager hands pressed between our knees.
Don't touch, we are warned, grandmother
turns the tiny brass key.

The polished objects, held within,
breathe out.

Vansittart Island

It frightened me as a child —
crowning on the horizon each morning,
bald as a drowned man's head.

A smooth, distant mass pointing
to some unnameable immensity.
Rising at dawn, its scattered corona of shipwrecks,
tilting black serifs.

We could see it through the kitchen window,
a perpetual breaching, hovering across the strait.

And each night that secret, rising nausea
of knowing it would be there again
come morning.

I knew even then
neither the warmth of the house,
its solid arms drawing the circle of family tight,
nor the reassuring smallness of childhood

could stave off
all the endings to come.

Keepsake

I told my uncle that I believed in ghosts,
so he asked me to define *ghost*.

I said a ghost was what remained
after something once living had died.

If that's your definition, he said, what about
the dead wood used to make your bed?
Does that have a ghost?

Or the animal skin
you wear on your feet as shoes?

The bone handled knife on your
bread and butter plate?

My skin began to prickle.
I looked about the room.

The wooden architraves
hummed a lament, husks of insects
flecking the windowsills
scuttled about my face.

That night, and for many nights thereafter,
I could not sleep for the ghostly embrace
of my dead bed, its timber frame
a composite of corpses,
sap run dry as a bled carcass.

And where, where would I be
after I died?

Caught in a limbo of dry bones,
or forever trapped, a trace of consciousness

in the handful of baby hair
shorn from my head by my mother

as a keepsake?

Hunger

Love wears thin at the end of the day
when her grandchildren join all the other
sucklings clamouring at her table for sustenance.

The stained tablecloth is a cartography of greed —
cats dip their paws in the cream bowl,
lick the salty pat of freshly-made butter.
Orphaned joeys crash among the cutlery,
sampling home produce, twitching mouths
neat as purses — black-tipped claws, nimble in the jam jar.

Spats break out over the tastiest morsels —
cats growl, joeys kick, plates crash to the floor.
Our grandmother roars, the beasts scatter —
paw prints and random droppings,

a stray whisker on a plate.

Night

Inside the Shearers hut
we make shadows with our hands.

My mother and brother laugh
as they conjure looming shapes.
Sinuous rabbits and long-nosed beasts,

the smell of candle wax — this makeshift
theatre, more exhilarating than cinema.
Above our roof, the dark firmament spins.

The bedroom is a warm green cocoon,
our three bodies prone on a soft broad bed.

Outside, cattle cast long shadows,
their mournful nocturnes break silence.
A lost key in a paddock gathers dew.

Fishing trawlers sweep the black waters,
the luminous spill from their floodlights
ruptures our dreams.

I am learning to love
what I cannot comprehend.

Day's End

Grandmother,
I used to follow you everywhere.

You brushed cobwebs from my path
while I cowered from orb spiders,
those poised, pointed stars at the centre of each taut net.

We gathered ripe apricots from the orchard.
Orange velvet and brown blemishes filled the bucket.
Apple cucumbers ripened on the vine,
fat as puffer fish.

You picked the paper lanterns of cape gooseberries,
gathered handfuls of pungent herbs, taught me
their names, marjoram, sage and thyme.

At day's end, your feet soaking
in a tub of steaming water, great swathes
of varicose veins roped around your calves
like the roots of ficus.
I averted my eyes.

The mantel clock chimed
as light sank beneath the horizon.
A thin plume rose
from your green glass teacup.

Gannet

Today she is snorkelling.
Her borrowed wetsuit,
a dark, billowing skin
she cannot fill.

As she enters the sea, something
thrashes at the water's edge.

Caught in a tourniquet of ribbon weed,
beak agape, its waterlogged
wingtips trawl water.

In the shallows they entwine.
Froth and spoiled feathers
cling to her wrists and shins.

Small hands cannot steer
these immense, sodden wings,
this breastbone so sharp and ragged.

Too late.

She is trapped inside
the searing stare,
a drowning bird's
blue eye.

Fright

My grandfather walked away across the howling paddocks.
Chest high in button grass, I was too small, flailing.

Above me a hard, bright sky, somewhere close,
the slow, hulking mountain of the bull's dark mass.

I called out in fright —

my voice,
a light puff of air.

Intimate apparel

My grandmother would never wear
a brassiere directly against her skin.
Instead she would fasten her bra
over two woollen singlets, as if
the peaks of her breasts were
wanton and unruly.

Swaddled in undergarments,
she appeared blockish, sexless.
Perhaps this was her intent –
cupping her breasts in lace might
reveal those shameful little udders
which pointed to some tender,
feminine place – porous,
suckled, desired.

Bide

Milk. The hot greasy substance of it —
spilling and swirling to the rhythm
of my grandmother's toil.
Each dawn the crooked stool and metal pail,
the greying apron. Her bent thumbs kneading
flesh, the teat's aperture opening — again, again.
Her square hand slapping the flank
of the restless goat, its hoof pounding dust.
My grandmother's high, wavering notes
floating across the milking yard —

The summer's gone, and all the roses falling.
        It's you, it's you, must go, and I must bide.

Packed lunch

I am eating the sandwich
my grandmother made me.
It's dry, full of pungent
home-made relish and hard cheese.
I am eating my grandmother. The crusts
of her affection catch in my throat. Her straight,
dry hair, firm high cheekbones. In my mouth,
the neat quarters of her nurturing,
piquant tang of intolerance.

I feel full — this meal is heavy.
Each mouthful, a mingling of ingredients;
her inventiveness, her cardigan — reeking
of goats and milking buckets. A trace of rancour,
shy hint of smile, clack, clack of ill-fitting dentures.
Accumulating inside me, her substance and songs,
the bright flare of her suspicious eyes.

It takes stamina to chew this sandwich.
Secretly, I yearn for something softer.
But you eat what you are given,
waste nothing.

The Final Night

She's waiting for the storm to pass,
and when it does, he must go.

His shoes are still under the bed,
quiet as breath. Her sleep is fitful.

Does she turn away from him this final night –
refuse to look upon the long white bag,
buckled loosely around his body –
the over-sized zipper, its staunch denial?

And when dawn comes,
does she turn towards him one last time,
say some private, tender thing?

Or does she silently rise from their bed –
comb her hair, pull on work clothes,

carry the brimming bucket
to the famished, waiting animals?

Beyond Reach

The leather recliners are cracked as dry heels,
cushions sunk with the weight of memory.

The clock chimes every hour,
the kitchen table waits.
In a drawer, serviettes grow brittle.
The tarnished cutlery is quiet.

Coiled on a hairbrush, my grandfather's
matted grey strands make a tiny creature
devoid of quiver or pulse.

In the bathroom cupboard, his razor, a cracked mug.
Empty overalls slack on a door hook.
In a pocket, his busy cursive on a small square
of notepaper mumbles to itself.

In my dream, the house is empty,
the warmth already gone from their bed.

In the highest, darkest corner of the pantry
my grandmother's voice is trapped in a jar,
her blustering rage preserved beyond reach.

The house is burning

Nothing will remain.
No voices, no fingerprints,
no well-worn impressions on linoleum.

The tracery of my grandparent's days,
the dusty, miniscule corners of their lives –
gone.

No hair-scent, no sweat.
No bedroom smells of warm bodies
and night animals.

The wooden drawers into which
my grandmother folded her practical clothes,
now tinder.

The clock has gone, the sideboard too.
All the glass teacups have exploded,
molten red rubies fizzing upon the pyre.

The blackened bones of the house
groan and buckle, each singular thing
now indistinguishable from the other.

Across the jet-black strait,
a night fishing vessel sees
only this –

one final point of light,
incandescent.

Archipelago

My head is an island,
my moods, scattered
archipelagos.

Family,
a bigger continent.

Shearwater burrows
pock my dunes,
secret runnels collapsing
my soft embankments.

Knots of clouds churn,
darkening my brilliant days.

I sing the dawn chorus,
rumble the low disgruntled
grunt of the stout grey goose.

Feel the grit of me,
the stony recesses.

I leak brackish tears.
Sooty tea trees sweep
the edges of my sad lagoons.

Growing up is an incoming tide,
a distant murmuration.

This island, a place
I must leave.

Eulogy

Launceston, 1974

This photograph was taken on the steps of our Great-great-grandmother's house. You and I are first cousins. I love you madly. You are a mysterious boy, vague and mercurial; I knock against you with my bony knees and my quick, changeable nature.

VITAMIN C

Upton Street, 1976

My family is visiting following the birth of your brother, Joshua. You greet me on the path at the side of your house with a palm full of orange vitamin C pills. "Here" you say, "try one of these, they're good for you!"

I am exhilarated at the concept of an orange, health-giving pill.

We enter the house, our mouths flooded with the synthetic flavour of orange.

In the tiny sloping sunroom baby is on the table having his nappy changed. I crane my head to see and find myself at eye-level with the black knot of his newly cut umbilical cord, fixed with an oversized plastic clamp. There is a strong smell of antiseptic and urine. I stare with a six-year old's curiosity as a slipstream of greenish tacky shit is wiped from the baby's florid little arse. The remains of a half-dissolved vitamin C tablet crumble in my mouth.

I can hear you breathing audibly through your nostrils with concentration; I look across at you to gauge your reaction – our eyes meet and we exchange a look of children's knowing.

*Crazy tired after a sleepover, we've crashed on the couch in our puffy
blue parkas, it's milk-and-biscuit time and we are both wrecked. Late
into the night we giggled, revelling in our private children's jokes.*

CARDBOARD BOX

Upton Street, 1977

We drag a large cardboard box to the dead end of the street where a steep median strip divides the road in two. A deep green pelt of grass with slippery potential covers the slope. We balance the box on the cusp of the incline and you, me and our baby brothers all climb in. Closing the cardboard flaps above us we chant *One, Two, Three!* Jerking our bodies forward, we propel our vessel forward and over the rise.

Down, down, down — we jolt and tumble blindly — then, smash! — we hit the road with fierce, ragged momentum. We all laugh helplessly inside the dark, sweet-smelling interior of the box, tangled together as if carelessly packaged.

You say, "Let's do it again." And our foreheads knock together as we nod in agreement.

At the height of summer we enjoy a tepid bath — my infant brother joins us. Their little boy genitals remind me of the cartoons I've seen advertising 'sea monkeys' — all wrinkled and primer pink.

COLOURING IN

Chifley St, 1978

We both love to draw and colour in. One weekend you are visiting – I get out my colour pencils and my new *Snow White and the Seven Dwarves* colouring book. I show you how to create contrast by shading the outer edge of a form with a darker colour and then filling the rest with lighter matching colour (a technique taught to me by my aunty).

I watch with incredulity as you repeatedly shade over the same spot on the page until the paper begins to thin and form little mealy balls like dead skin. A hole finally forms in the paper, which you keep scratching with your fingernails. I have a violent urge to cry. I find your colouring-in technique childish and irrational.

A week later you send me a drawing you have made of a green paddock done in thick oil pastels. It's a simple drawing – a big slab of dense green, a scratchy little line to suggest a fence and a flat, impossibly blue sky. Looking at it, I am suffused by an acute sense of wellbeing. The colouring-in incident is forgiven.

At a family gathering we pose for a photo; I've placed my arm on my brother's head, you are checking to see if you've copied the gesture correctly. This is how it is with us; I lead, you follow.

SUNBATHING

Chifley Street, 1979

I am sunbathing on the balcony when you arrive at my house. I am feeling very sophisticated in my brown and white striped bathers, and you, possessing only a pair of Bonds cotton underpants, are reticent to join me in the sun. "Come on," I say, "the sun is out, no one will care."

I coerce you into stripping down to your undies and joining me on the cement patio. I stretch out in the sun; you sit hunched, folding and intertwining your thin arms in an attempt to cover your little boy's bony body, all ribs and elbows. Eventually your shyness convinces me that there must be something lewd about your pale torso and your gaping underpants.

When dad appears with a camera, we smile and I hide my strange sense of disquiet beneath a snapshot attitude.

BIG TEETH

Launceston, 1980

You are jealous of my second teeth. Whenever I visit you take me into the garden behind the pampas grass and ask if you can see them. You peel back my lips and scrutinise my gums. You prod at the holes left by my departing milk teeth and run a finger over the buds of the new teeth erupting through the gums. Then you run your finger along your own gums. You have long pink gums and very petite teeth.

"It's not fair," you say, "I want big teeth like yours." I feel obscurely proud, touched by your ardent appreciation.

Around this time, you suffer a bout of intestinal worms. At night you complain of an itching anus. Each night your mother creeps into your room with a torch, peels back layers of bedding and parts the cheeks of your buttocks. There, in the beam of the torch she sees white tapeworms writhing in the light. She calls her husband and together they watch the little parasitic circus while you sleep on, oblivious.

Whenever I see you, I visualise this gentle nocturnal violation.

Beside the fragrant hedges of lavender and the sundial, we pause reluctantly mid-game for a Kodak moment.

DRAWING

St Helens, 1981

We have not seen each other for a few months. When we meet again, a few things have changed; the easy rapport we had in early childhood has gone. Your parents have divorced and you are testing a new belligerence. You are angry and displaced.

Elongated and pre-pubescent, you are much more guarded than you were. You and I are suddenly aware of our genders and a prickly new distance arises between us. It was never like this before.

You are staying with us at the holiday home in St Helens – your little brother, mother and her new boyfriend accompany you. Your mother is in courtship mode and you feel left out. She prepares pasta carbonara with red wine for her new lover while you and your brother eat plain ham sandwiches in a separate room.

Our little brothers pair up and we are left to re-negotiate our new status as strangers. It's awkward – until we start to make a drawing together. On a large piece of butcher's paper we create a science fiction drawing with an apocalyptic burning city, space ships, hostile aliens – and a foreboding scarlet sky. We are utterly absorbed in our drawing and spend hours on it. Every day for a week we spread the paper out on the kitchen floor and commence painting. Even during a violent thunderstorm (your Airedale terrier, Bertie, cowering under the kitchen table in terror), we quietly paint on.

By the time our holiday is up the drawing is three quarters finished – we smile at one another and promise we'll finish it another time.

Sitting beside our Grandfather's infamous woodpile, we smile self-consciously for the camera. You are suffering hayfever and clutch a single white tissue. I am stroking Bertie the Airedale Terrier...

SPIDER

October, 1981

You tripped on your shoelace while crossing the road. You fell; a car came over the rise and ran-over you. Your little brother was there — he witnessed everything. You were ten years old.

In your top pocket you carried a pet huntsman. At the scene of the accident your little brother retrieved the dead spider from your pocket. He watched the spider vigilantly for signs of life many days after you died.

I remember its dark, lifeless legs tumbling open on the palm of his hand as he repeated, *"But I did see it move - look!"*

My world took on uncomfortable new angles. Everything felt like a bad dream. All my interactions felt artificial, school felt surreal and my mother became unfamiliar to me in her state of grieving.

I vividly recall that first night after receiving the news — lying in bed willing sleep to take me but feeling corrupted, knowing something irreversible had happened. I couldn't quite believe that you were dead.

Everything around me had brittleness about it — reality felt paper-thin. And like the drawing you had once coloured-in, a dark, ragged hole had been torn open on a page of our lives.

BLIZZARD

Melbourne, 2006

Sometimes I wonder who you might have been. You would be thirty-five now. I didn't attend your funeral. I recall overhearing my Aunt describing the 'viewing' "They'd done such a good job tidying him up," she said, "he looked very peaceful." Grandad said, "One eye was almost gone and he had a little smile on his face."

As a young teenager I was haunted by images of you in your coffin.

In my mind's eye you just lay there, eyes open, unable to decompose. You were pristine; a boy in a 1970's pullover suspended for all eternity between oblivion and adulthood. I came to associate you with the smell of wet bitumen and the sensation of biting on aluminium foil. My heart stung like a thousand paper cuts.

After you died I was offered our unfinished holiday drawing. I looked at it briefly — it hurt so much I never looked again.

In my heart you will always be the boy who gave me a brown polished gemstone when I was seven; the boy who lived in a large rambling house with an antique barber's chair in the sunroom and a maze of cool rooms. You drew exceptional spaceships.

In the backyard we climbed the almond tree, cut our fingers on pampas grass and teased our little brothers. We had a special rapport, you and me.

In a sense my ten-year-old self has, like yours, ceased to exist. We both belong in the realm of memory; only, I have had the opportunity to look back at the history we shared.

Therryn, you were my first cousin and my first love lost.

After your death we were given some snapshots of you taken during a skying holiday – you loved the snow. There you stand in a white world, almost erased. Memory too, is like a vast snowfield – recollection fading to white with the long, irrevocable blizzard of time.

Keening

Whenever it rains

I think of dead things.
The broken slick of cormorant feather –
disarticulated wing, snagged on sea wrack.
Constellations of smashed snails after downpour.
My old departed dog buried somewhere
in an unknown field. I think of the dead like hail-battered
daisies knocked down and becoming more
the substance of bruise than matter.

A friend visits.
We talk of our fear of death, she begins to cry.
Tears streak her cheeks, she blinks her dark eyes –
the same kind of startle I have seen in the eyes
of other living things. I do not say consoling words,
they hint at condescension.
Instead, I hug her, say
I'm glad you were born.

Outside, the rain.

Glove Puppets

I have grown ambivalent towards them.

The puppet boy has a 1950s side parting
a cocked, conspiratorial eyebrow.
His fixed, impish grin verges on perversion.

Who made his little garment? It's garish —
a yellow rose print and spotted sleeves,
the repurposed scrap of a sundress.

The German girl has hooded blue eyes.
Her cinnamon bun hairstyle is an Aryan shade,
demure smile shows no teeth.

Whose hand slipped inside her polka-dot frock,
to animate her? Who assumed her voice,
its churlish tones and puppet squeaks?

These fossilised cartoons hover on the shelf,
arms open as if surrendering — empty handed.
Perhaps it's a gesture of perpetual optimism,

opening to childhood as it comes around
again and again. But once for you and me,
in perpetuity for these vinyl effigies.

When I am dead and buried, they will still be
grinning somewhere, cloth arms pitched wide,
glove bodies soliciting for the borrowed vitality

of another's fingers.

After the Fire

Dunalley 2013

She sends me an envelope.
Inside, photos of charred porcelain faces,
remnants of her mothers china dolls.
No note, no explanation —
just singed, cherubic faces with grey lips
and hollow, ash-rimmed eyes.

She's pulled their little white heads and hands from
the charnel ground of her incinerated house,
stitched them back together with twine and glue.

Crowned with garlands of she-oak and marram grass,
they have necklaces of scallop shell and beach glass.
Heads propped on empty bottles, their ashen forearms
and smudged hands dangle by their sides.

These postcards frighten me.

I am like these dolls, she says —
a terrible, blackened survivor lost in this world.

Rising

Above us soared the ruined staircase
and attic rooms, still wallpapered
in delicate pastels.

The sandstone walls were crumbling,
the floor completely gone.
Only fresh-trodden earth
and manure of sheltering cows
beneath our feet.

I spied it in a corner,
delicate as a fallen moth,

a tender filament
between this time and another,
brilliant, yet unassuming.

A maroon silk dome,
the remnant of a lady's bonnet —
small as a puckered breast,
a single button at its centre,
broken black lace trailing one edge.

I held it in the palm of my hand,
felt its softness and silence —

but this tiny silken crown,
risen from the churned black clay
was not mine to keep.

So I set her high
on an empty windowsill
overlooking what remained
of her sunlit dominion.

The Fact

It flew from me and lodged somewhere
in the ceiling beam –

my terror, a small eruption, sharp as shrapnel.
Embedded in a knot of wood, its dark brown
foreboding holding up the roof.

I looked across to where you lay,
ear folded against a pillow,
the disordered fan of your cowlick, radiant –

I do not want
to die, I whispered.

No one does, you said.

Above us, detaching from the beam,
a cobweb – diaphanous
in morning light.

How softly it fell.

Keening

When I was young, death was something
that happened to other people.

Now I've scattered dry ashes, longed for lost voices —
how to grieve such startling acts of disappearance?

~

I think of my old dog, whose muscles quivered after death,
the body's last, stubborn striving for existence.

As the vet lifted her from my arms a thin stream of urine
poured from her onto my lap — I laughed incongruously.

~

These, my dear departed, are simply and resoundingly
gone — a void I did not anticipate.

~

At the bottom of the paddock stood two old sandstone tombs,
names completely obliterated by gunshot and weather.

Those pocked, bald stones could only hold their expressions
of grief for so long before collapsing into erasure —

around them, marram grass tall as a man,
that wind, fierce as long forgotten keening.

~

The Hungry Air

Summers we stayed in an old fibro shack.
It had a front door that opened   onto
a non-existent verandah   and missing stairs.

In the kitchen was a tin   inside, old playing cards
decorated with white carousel horses
                    on an aquamarine background.

They smelled of old money and nicotine,
but were of unparalleled beauty   their milky manes
and broken golden borders diffuse   beneath a film of grime.

The shack was musty   heavy with   the aroma
of wet, sandy towels.   My brother and I slept on twin beds,
coral and jade coloured mattresses   from the 1940s.

At night, I felt the mattress buttons pressing   into my thin back
as I listened   to my brother's fitful dreaming.

My parents   slept in a corner bedroom
piled with suitcases and stale pyjamas   dreams of separation.

The shack stood on coarse sandy soil   beneath a small hill.
The hill   was a place of   exhilarating mystery.
In the corners   of my vision   shadows quivered,

spiders scuttled,   retreating   into tunnels,
          snapping trapdoors shut behind them.

Ants trailed sparkling quartz gravel in single file.
All around me, cicadas   pulsing song of tea tree and heat.

As an adult, I returned.   The shack had gone, only
                a concrete tank stand remained.

Where once I had stood, just six years old,
                now a woman —
                                the hungry air.

Acknowledgements

Some of these poems or versions of these poems have been published in *Australian Poetry Journal, Foam:e #14, Tincture Journal, Southerly, Transnational Literature, The Sleepers Almanac* and *Communion*.

Heartfelt thanks to Maurice, Anna, Emilie, Alana & Ross with whom I have workshopped poetry over the past few years. You have taught me so much and given me the confidence to offer my writing to others.

And finally, to Andy who has been a patient and formative presence in my life, thank you for your generosity, love and keen insight.

About the author

Rachael Wenona Guy creates writing, performance and visual art. She creates puppet-based, visual theatre for adults and collaborative multi-media installations examining memory, embodiment and identity.

Her creative writing has been published in journals and online within Australia and internationally. In 2015 she was shortlisted for the Whitmore Poetry Manuscript prize.

rimofacup.wordpress.com